SUCCESSFUL PARENTING:

RESTORING LOST VALUES IN A MODERN WORLD

James Theros

LEVEL 10 PUBLISHING

Successful Parenting: Restoring Lost Values in a Modern World
Copyright © 2010-2019 by James Theros.

Copies of this book may be purchased for educational, business, or sales promotional use. For more information, please write or email:

Level 10 Publishing
33863 US Highway 19 N.
Palm Harbor, FL 34684
MasterTheros@Yahoo.com

THIRD EDITION

Book design by JustYourType.biz

Library of Congress Cataloging-in-Publication Data
Successful Parenting: Restoring Lost Values in a Modern World,
Third edition, James Theros

ISBN 978-0-615-36473-9

CONTENTS

✧

Foreword v

Preface..vii

Chapter One
Yesterday's Values. Why Have They Changed and
Where Have They Gone? 1

Chapter Two
Being the Parent You Wanted as a Child 7

Chapter Three
The Value of Organized Activities................................13

Chapter Four
The Value of Expectations 31

Chapter Five
The Value of Mental Programming................................39

Chapter Six
The Value of Learning to Lose....................................51

Chapter Seven
The Value of Self-Defense Training................................55

Chapter Eight
The Value of Coping with Peer Pressure..........................63

Chapter Nine
The Value of Integrity..69

Chapter Ten
The Value of Financial Responsibility..................................73

Chapter Eleven
The Value of Arriving Early and Staying Late...................75

Chapter Twelve
The Value of Reading 79

Chapter Thirteen
The Value of Setting Goals..83

Chapter Fourteen
The Value of Being a Parent First 89

The Ten Articles of Mental Training 94

Children's Home Rules 95

The Student Creed.. 96

Afterword 97

FOREWORD

✧

I wrote this book because of the unique opportunity of being a martial arts instructor. As such, I have been able to witness the results of using the suggestions presented in this book.

And, thanks to social media, I've been able to observe the results of different parenting methods. I believe that the suggestions offered here can be of great help to anyone seeking a better future for their child.

Throughout the book, I will refer to martial arts training. I will be sharing how what we do in our program can work for any parent seeking better results at home or school.

Having a child involved in a good traditional martial arts program can make a huge difference in their lives, which is due to the inherent personal development aspects of the martial arts.

I will also be sharing some stories from my crazy childhood to help illustrate points. I hope you will find them entertaining as well as informative.

I commend you for taking the time to read a book like this because it shows that you care about your child's future.

PREFACE

✦

The Foundation of my Beliefs

I was born in 1969. My mother was only 20 years old, and since I was her first child, I was something of an experiment for her.

My younger brother was born exactly 20 months later.

When I was five years old, my parents divorced, and it wasn't long before another man came into the picture; the first of two men who would become my stepfathers.

After my mother remarried, I can still remember telling my first-grade teacher that my last name had changed. At the time, I didn't realize that because my mother's last name had changed that mine had not.

Ralph was a construction worker when I met him and later became a truck driver.

He had come from a low place in life. He had been to prison, and fathered three kids; two of them were in and out of jail regularly.

His youngest son, Michael, came to live with us after getting expelled from high school for frequent fighting and disrespect issues.

He was a very large 15-year old but carried himself more like an adult.

Due to my parent's work schedules, Michael was in charge of caring for my brother and me during the week. To a couple of little kids like us, he was the coolest person on the planet.

He introduced us to cigarettes, marijuana, pornography, and profanity. He owned a handgun and hung out with unsavory friends who looked like the kinds of guys you'd see in gangster movies.

My brother and I felt safe around him because he could hold his own with anyone.

He seemed educated in a great many things. Unfortunately, reading, writing, and arithmetic weren't among them.

He was usually kind to us, but he also became the bullying big brother once in a while, too.

On one such occasion, Michael held me up in the front window of our townhouse (with only my underwear on) to display me to all the neighbor kids.

I got teased about it for weeks afterward.

I was also getting bullied at school. My mother even had to leave work early one day to confront the school administrators about the issue.

In 2nd grade, I attended an arts and crafts class, where I made a little hand-puppet that looked like a dog.

I created it from an empty milk carton. We used orange construction paper to give it color. We then glued on ears and eyes and made it as life-like as possible. I had worked very hard on it and was quite proud of the finished product. I couldn't *wait* to take it home to show it to my mother.

On the bus ride home, my friend Jimmy asked to hold it. When I didn't allow him to, he got upset and threatened to beat me up as soon as we got off the bus.

True to his word, as soon as we stepped off the bus, he immediately punched me and snatched the puppet from me. He made fun of it, and then stomped on it; destroying it before I could show it to my mother.

I never forgot that incident, and Jimmy and I had frequent fights over it, afterward. Our battles usually ended up with me running home crying.

When I decided that I didn't want to ride the bus home anymore, another incident occurred.

My brother and I were leaving school for the day, and two boys began taunting us, looking to start a fight.

The smaller of the two noticed I was wearing a watch and told the other to take it from me.

The bigger one grabbed my arm and held it still while the other removed the watch. My brother and I stood there, helpless; unsure of how to respond.

The boys made some other disparaging remarks and then tossed my watch over the bridge and into the creek.

They pushed me around for another minute, attempting to get me to fight, but I was too scared to act.

When we arrived home, I told Ralph about the incident.

I was looking for some sympathy (or an impromptu boxing lesson) from him. Instead, he made light of it and suggested that I should have punched the boy in the nose.

In hindsight, that might not have been such bad advice.

Finally, though, a solution came in the form of an after school program.

There were various activities to choose from; origami, tennis, football, basketball, soccer, chess club, creative writing, etc.

One of the activities was Karate.

Something inside told me that this was for me, so I took the registration form home and asked my mother about it.

She signed the form for me, but when I returned it, they told me that the class was already full.

I was heartbroken but decided to do the origami class instead. Then the incident with the little orange cardboard dog happened.

It was at that point that I realized I needed this class more than I knew.

When the next session began, they *again* told me that the class was full.

This time though, another boy had gotten nervous at the last minute and dropped out, which left an opening for me.

When they told me that I was in, I almost floated to the ceiling.

In my first class, I recognized one of my good friends wearing a clean, white, pressed Karate uniform. And, he was already a brown belt!

I had no idea that my friend Dennis was even learning Karate at all.

It was common at that time to keep martial arts training a secret because the element of surprise gave a martial artist an added advantage in a self-defense situation.

The Sensei (teacher) was a very confident looking, middle-aged, African-American woman. She had piercing brown eyes and a very stoic face.

She spoke in a calm voice as she explained how the training would benefit us if we took it seriously.

Next, she asked if anyone would like to be a volunteer.

Not one to pass up an opportunity, I raised my hand.

She asked me to come to the center of the circle that we were sitting in and, to my delight, called Dennis out with me.

I was grinning from ear to ear!

You see, Dennis and I were playmates at school who got separated at least once per day for acting silly together.

Something in Dennis' eyes looked different this time, though.

There was no silly smile to meet mine. Dennis was completely focused and serious and made no direct eye contact.

Back in those days, to dispel any doubts, martial arts training began with a sparring match to prove to the uninitiated how effective the art was.

The instructor asked us to bow to each other and assume a fighting stance.

I turned towards her with a look of puzzlement as I had no idea what to do. She ignored me, looked at Dennis, and yelled, "Go!"

All I can remember past that was the searing pain that I felt in my left thigh from the repeated roundhouse kicks, delivered by my friend Dennis.

I never even got to move.

I fell to the floor, in tears, while the class looked at me in astonishment.

I did my best to collect myself.

My leg hurt like crazy, but I became immediately hooked!

I couldn't wait for each new class to begin and I practiced every day at home between lessons.

I rushed off to the school library and checked out the only books available on martial arts at the time; one about Karate, the other about Judo.

I read them from cover to cover so many times that I could recite every word by memory.

I remember trying out the Judo throws on my brother. For some reason, he was willing to let me attempt to throw him over my shoulder (which I could never quite do).

One evening, my mother came home and told me that she had met a co-worker who taught martial arts at an actual Karate school. She told me that she'd convinced him to let me try a few classes.

I ended up training there long enough to earn my first belt; and I was excited about the next leg of the journey.

Then my world came crashing down.

My mother informed me that I would not be continuing due to the cost.

As my quest to learn continued, a friend introduced me to a guy who had some experience in Kung Fu.

He was only 5 or 6 years older than me and offered to teach me in his back yard. He had a very cool, James Dean-like demeanor about him. The way he moved was impressive, and I wanted those skills, too.

I headed to his house in the mornings to learn from him for a year or two.

His training helped me handle a few self-defense encounters, but I longed to be part of a real martial arts school again.

My prayers were soon answered one day while walking across the way to browse the toys at a popular store. As I was leaving the store, I noticed a small Asian man dressed in a peach-colored silk Kung Fu uniform. He was practicing some weapons on the sidewalk several doors down.

I watched as he displayed remarkable skill that I had only seen in movies.

When he noticed me watching, he stopped, smiled, and asked if I had an interest in learning martial arts.

He had only recently opened his school in the plaza and only had a handful of students. There were pictures in the windows of him doing high-flying kicks and other things that any teenage boy would find amazing. My excitement must have been palpable. He handed me a flyer that talked about Karate, Kung Fu, Meditation, and Philosophy.

The flyer mentioned that he had over 35 years' experience and that he had trained many champions.

I thanked him, took the flyer, and *sprinted* home to talk to my stepfather about it. I begged him to take me back so he could meet the man.

After a lot of badgering from me, Ralph drove me back to the school to speak to the master.

He asked a few questions about the training and then asked how much lessons would cost. Ralph told the master he'd think about it and get back with him.

At home, he told me that he would sign the paperwork for me, but I'd have to find a way to pay for it myself.

With my head lowered, I entered the school again and relayed the message that I couldn't afford to enroll.

The master must have seen the heartbreak in my eyes. He made a special offer that would allow me to enroll, as long as my parents would be willing to sign the agreement.

I had recently gotten a paper route and was to pay him whatever I could afford (which usually amounted to my dumping a few rolls of coins on his desk each week).

He also tasked me with passing out flyers and cleaning the school before and after classes.

I fell in love with the training and with my Master's persona. His words of wisdom began to change me from the inside out.

Master Choi always had high expectations of me. These expectations, coupled with his belief in me, helped me during a period of significant instability in my life.

The lessons I learned from him went well beyond the physical techniques. His philosophy on life was what affected me the most.

I learned a great deal about how to mentor and nurture others. Master Choi taught me the skills of leadership that have continued to serve me decades later.

What a different path my life would have taken had I not met this man on that fateful day in 1983.

Many of the things that make a great martial arts teacher also make a great parent. And these are the concepts I will be sharing throughout this book.

✧

CHAPTER ONE

Yesterday's Values: Why Have They Changed and Where Have They Gone?

In the early days of our country, entire communities participated in the raising of the youth. The mantra, "It takes a village to raise a child" was the philosophy of the time.

If a child was disrespectful to a neighbor, parents would take the child over and have them apologize.

It was commonplace to have someone "other" than a child's parents correct them if they misbehaved.

This philosophy seems to be missing from today's society. Kids don't appear to be getting taught to respect their elders as before. Unfortunately, the kids will grow up one day, and then it will be *their* turn to be the elders.

Let's turn back the clock to the latter half of the 1960s for a moment to see where this all started.

The "Happy Days" that were the 1950s were long gone, and there was a new shift in the culture. Teens and young adults were experimenting with hallucinogenic drugs and free love.

The great counter-culture had begun, and their mantra was "sex, drugs and rock 'n roll."

It was a time of great turmoil in our country.

The long-standing Vietnam War was going on, and there were many protests and riots. The young adults of that generation grew distrustful and resentful of leadership and authority figures of the day. Rebellion became a constant theme.

Additionally, the kids of that time had grown up in a more-prosperous time than their parents (who lived through the Great Depression). This group of kids (who would later become parents) came to be known as "The Baby Boomers."

It was a time in our country's history when the population was made up of more kids than adults. It was common for families to have 5-10 kids per household. My mother was one of 11!

I can only imagine how challenging it must have been to have been a parent of that many kids and how difficult it had to be to keep everything under control.

The parents of the Baby Boomers were known as "The Greatest Generation; due, in large part, to the levels of hardship they endured during their childhoods.

The baby boomers did not experience the same hardships. Thus, they had a very different view on how the world worked, and began the gradual softening of their kids.

Without the same foundational childhoods of our grandparents, our country's morals and values began to shift.

Much of this newer generation questioned anything coming from the mouths of authority figures. This included politicians, police officers, teachers...and *their parents.*

Many of the younger parents of that generation developed a different thought process when it came to the whole, "*It takes a village to raise a child*" mentality of *their* parents.

As such, it became more common for parents to confront other adults attempting to correct their children's misbehavior.

Rather than allowing others to help keep the kids in the neighborhood under control, parents began telling others to mind their own business.

I can remember my mother scolding our neighbors (and some of the faculty members at my elementary school) for correcting my brother and me; even when we deserved it. She always took our side, and we learned how to use that to our advantage.

All we needed was to tell our mother that a neighbor got on us for being too loud, and she sprang into action in our defense.

While she may have meant well, it only put the actual authority into our hands (the kids), and that's pretty much where it's been since.

Additionally, in my early childhood, teachers paddled children who misbehaved in class. It may surprise you to learn that I was no stranger to that paddle.

When a classmate got paddled, they always came back into the classroom with tears in their eyes and improved behavior. The other kids took note, and behaved much better, too.

Then, a court case (*Ingraham vs. Wright*) in 1977 began challenging the right of teachers to paddle children when they misbehaved.

Some parents felt that teachers didn't have the right to put their hands on their kids, for *any* reason.

Kids today *know* that teachers are not allowed to paddle or physically discipline them.

School bus drivers have also been greatly affected by this change in our societal values. There are countless news stories of bus drivers lashing out after being repeatedly marginalized by the kids on their bus.

Today, teachers' and bus drivers' hands are tied, and the kids know it. With the abundance of cameras, we have been witness to how kids have taken advantage of it.

The court system has put the authority into the hands of the kids. When a case goes to court, the children rarely appear to be at fault.

It has also become commonplace to have social services called on parents who spank their kids.

One other often-overlooked reason for the decline in children's behavior has been the increase in having both parents in the workforce, leaving the task of raising the child to others.

So this begs the question, "Are any of yesteryear's morals and values still around?"

Fortunately, the answer is, "Yes;" if you look carefully.

And, one of these places you can still find some of these old-school morals and values is in the traditional martial arts.

You may have to do some searching, because this new-age mentality has found its way into the martial arts, as well.

Some schools have lowered their standards to keep from losing students (and the revenue they bring in).

That said, I have always said that there are three things that every child should have to do by the time they are an adult:

1. Serve in the military.

2. Work in a fast-food restaurant.

3. Earn a black belt in the martial arts.

Serving in the military will mold their character by teaching them about teamwork and attention to detail; as well as giving them a sense of pride in their country.

Working in a fast-food restaurant will teach them the basics of customer service (something sorely lacking today); and will show them what drudgery is like if they don't make better choices now.

Earning a black belt in a traditional martial art will help them develop a confident, respectful attitude; and a multitude of other traits, as well.

Doctors and psychologists often recommend traditional martial arts training for kids due to the combination of physical exercise and behavior modifications (aka morals and values).

Also, in traditional martial arts training, there is a measure of mental, spiritual, and emotional training that can be lacking in other activities.

Since martial arts is a year-round activity, there is plenty of time to teach the applications of *life skills* that go far beyond the martial arts training floor.

It's a well-known fact that many professional athletes supplement their sports training with traditional martial arts training.

CHAPTER TWO

✧

Being the Parent You Needed as a Child

Pay now or pay later. Those are your only two options as a parent.

If you do the work required to raise a child with proper morals and values, that's the *pay now* mindset. Just know upfront that it's not always going to be easy or convenient. Parenting is a fulltime job, and it's downright tough sometimes!

If not, you'll end up paying later; and paying *for* it might be a better choice of words.

Your job is to be the parent that you needed when *you* were growing up.

Give your kids the feeling of stability, safety, security, and *unconditional* love.

Make healthy choices for your kids and <u>don't allow them to have much say in the matter.</u>

Great parents enforce good grooming habits even though their kids may fuss about it.

And, since you're a great parent, you enforce these and other things as well.

If allowed to, kids will make decisions based on how they *feel* at the moment. Seldom will they take time to think about the long-term repercussions of their choices.

And, in the end, life is a series of choices and decisions.

Great parents teach their kids how to make good choices and decisions, and help make it a habit to continue doing so.

It's important to set firm boundaries with your child.... and then don't budge.

Kids intrinsically know there are boundaries, but their mission is to see just how far they can stretch them. Kids are little code-breakers.

So, it's essential to be consistent; otherwise, your child will receive mixed messages.

An informative yet straightforward example is when your child asks for something at the store that they don't need.

They ask mom and hear no. Mom then proceeds to have an argument with her child over the decision.

The child continues whining to get her way, and, if she gets it, she's just *broken the code*.

She now has a proven formula to get her way in the future.

Here's a better suggestion when this situation occurs:

Inform your child that if they continue asking you will take away a privilege. It could be dessert, playing with their friends, playing games, or whatever else they most want.

If you stand firm with your decision, the child learns that you have *firm* boundaries.

If you ground your child, stick to it. Sticking to it teaches your child that you mean business.

Resist the urge to relent in any way. Set up the rules beforehand.

You may even consider creating a chart that shows what the punishment will be for the *crimes* they commit.

For example, what will happen if they get caught lying?

Will they be grounded? Will they lose some other privilege?

Let them see it in writing so they're not surprised by it and you don't have to think about how to respond.

What will happen if they get caught arguing or fighting with their sibling? Put it in writing.

How about if they don't do what you ask them the first time? The second time? The third time?

A chart like the one on the next page can be used the next time your child acts up. Take the concept and let your imagination run wild.

CONGRATULATIONS!
YOU GOT GROUNDED!!

To get ungrounded, you must earn 500 points

○ Write a nice letter to someone in the family=10 points _____

○ Write a nice letter to a neighbor=10 points _____

○ Help a relative with homework=20 points _____

○ Prepare and cook dinner=50 points _____

○ 1 load of laundry (wash, dry, fold and put away)=100 points _____

○ Clean and organize a kitchen cupboard=50 points
per cupboard _____

○ Empty dishwasher=25 points _____

○ Clean and wash off table=25 points _____

○ Clean and wash off counters=25 points _____

○ Wash kitchen chairs=25 points _____

○ Clean out microwave=40 points _____

○ Take out garbage and re-bag=10 points _____

○ Scrub bathroom sink=10 points _____

○ Takeout bathroom trash=10 points _____

○ Clean toilet=50 points _____

○ Water plants=25 points _____

○ Clean and vacuum living room=30 points _____

○ Dust living room=50 points _____

○ Wash windows in living room and kitchen= 50 points _____

○ Sweep and mop kitchen floor=25 points _____

View yourself as a police officer of sorts who enforces the laws in your home. When citizens misbehave, they receive a warning, a ticket, or even *jail* time.

Word to the wise: Your child may try to manipulate you by going behind your back to your significant other in an attempt to overturn your decision.

Communicate in advance to your significant other that if your child asks for something that you will always ask if they have already spoken to the other parent.

"If your dad said no already, then that's the answer. End of discussion."

Resist the urge to demean your significant other in front of the child. If you have issues, handle them privately. In the martial arts, we call this Public Praise, Private Reprimand.

If you undermine your significant other in front of your child, know that it will affect their ability to parent effectively.

Kids need to know that their parents are *in charge*. Demeaning your significant other in front of your kids will only serve to cause them to see the other parent as "one of the kids."

I wish it weren't true, but this happened in our household regularly. My brother and I learned to use it to our advantage with our stepfather. It caused a lot of problems that could have been avoided had our parents communicated a little more.

CHAPTER THREE

✧

The Value of Organized Activities

M any activities have a trial program to determine the interest-level of a child before having them commit to it long term.

Most martial arts programs today require students to be in classes twice per week. Therefore, it doesn't have to be as time-consuming as some other activities.

For parents looking to give their child a real edge in life, martial arts should be on the list of activities to consider.

Traditional martial arts training helps kids develop strong morals and values more than virtually any other activity.

Here's why traditional martial arts training has so much to offer to children. Mentally, they will develop skills in these areas:

• Respect (respecting themselves, others, and authority figures)

• Focus (learning to block out distractions)

• Discipline (developing the ability to do what they should be doing without having to be told)

- Self-Control (learning to refrain from doing things that they shouldn't do)

- Patience (learning to be willing to wait or to take their time on projects)

- Modesty (learning not to brag about themselves)

- Honesty (learning to be honest with themselves and with others)

- Perseverance (learning to develop resilience and stick-to-it-iveness)

- Indomitable Spirit (learning never to allow challenges to conquer them)

- Confidence (learning that they can do anything they put their mind to)

- Mental/Emotional Strength (learning how to cope with fears and doubts and handle stress)

- Increased Social Skills (learning to make friends and get along with others)

- Leadership Skills (learning to mentor and lead, which looks GREAT on a college application)

- Physically, they will develop skills in these areas:

- Exercise

- Coordination

- Stamina

- Flexibility

- Strength

- Speed

- Agility

- Self-Defense Ability

And, while I'm sure that other activities might offer some of these same things, I'm not convinced that any provides them all.

It's important to note, however, that not all martial arts programs are the same.

Some of them approach the training purely as a sport, while others approach it from the self-defense aspect. Still others (like ours) are more of a continuing-education program, where the focus is on personal development.

Additionally, martial arts is one of the few activities that kids and parents can do *together*. Talk about family bonding!

QUITTING

When your child wants to quit an activity, it can become an essential teachable moment that you can use to help your child develop a critical mental muscle that will benefit them for the rest of their lives.

The muscle I'm referring to is their *perseverance muscle.*

Children will develop their perseverance muscle or their *quit* muscle.

And guess what? It's primarily up to *you* which muscle you permit to grow stronger.

If you let *them* choose, they're going to take the path of least resistance. The pressures they feel may go away, but their progress will go away, too.

And, once everything settles down, it will become challenging to get going again.

I've never heard a child thank a parent later for letting them quit something as a child.

If you can see the benefits of having your child continue with an activity, don't be afraid to pull the "parent card" and keep them going. Trust me when I say they will thank you for it later.

Perseverance and dedication are habits. Unfortunately, so is quitting.

If you allow your child to quit activities based on how they feel at the moment, this may show up later on when they have the choice to drop out of college, change careers, or even end a marriage before attempting to work things out.

Expect your child to persevere and he will. Remind your child that everyone wants to quit sometimes, even champions.

The difference between the champions (and everyone else) is that they never *act* on the desire to quit.

High confidence comes from overcoming obstacles. Anytime a challenging goal is set, there will be obstacles. Once again, this is one of the areas where traditional martial arts training can help.

In the martial arts (as with so many other areas in life) some of the more-common obstacles are:

- Fear & Doubt

- Illness & Injuries

- Boredom

- Conflicts with Playtime

- Lack of Progress

Students who go on to achieve their black belts learn to deal with each of these obstacles. We spend a great deal of time teaching them healthy ways to handle each one.

FEAR AND DOUBT

Kids are naturally going to have fears, and we teach students that experiencing fear is part of being human. However, giving in to their fear is a *choice*. We provide them with a safe place to test their mental and physical skills (the Dojang/Dojo) so that they can overcome those fears and doubts.

We let them know that failing is ok; and that we *expect* it.

One of the things that draw great parents to our program is that we don't automatically pass every student who tests.

Students in our program know that if they haven't developed the skills needed to pass, they will have to reset their goal and try again. Just like they are already doing in their favorite video game.

We teach them that when they fail, we expect them to try again. We climb inside students' minds and address their possible thought-processes *before* it happens for real.

We call it *Chil Jun Pal Gi* (Fall Down 7, Get Up 8).

When kids doubt their abilities, we help them see that it's mostly in their minds. Our instructors (and their classmates) work together to assure them that they can do much more than they initially think they can.

In fact, on average, those who achieve their black belt will have wanted to quit at least three times.

It's the process of *working through their challenges* that helps them achieve the benefits of martial arts that we hear so much about.

Without these moments of struggle, nothing happens. It's all part of the process.

Imagine a movie like *Rocky*, or *The Karate Kid* without the struggle (what we call "Act 3"). How much less inspiring would those movies or characters be if they had no struggle?

To illustrate how this can play out, I'll use an actual situation that took place at our school.

A single mother enrolled her 9-year-old son with the hopes that we could help him deal with some anger issues. His father had left when he was very young, and the boy blamed his mother as the cause.

He was a very respectful, happy young man who thoroughly enjoyed classes. He wanted to come to class every day, and he always arrived early to practice on his own.

One evening I overheard his mother, asking him to hurry up because she needed to get him home.

He ignored her and continued practicing, avoiding eye contact with his mother.

She repeated herself to which he replied, *"I'm not ready yet."*

I heard this from my office and stepped out to address the situation.

His mother shrugged her shoulders and looked at me, uncertain about what to do next.

I approached the boy and asked him to repeat what his mother had asked him.

"She said it was time to go, sir."

"Then why aren't you changing your clothes and getting ready to leave?" I asked.

He attempted the same reply with me, *"Because I'm not ready to, sir."*

I then said in a firm tone, *"Go change your clothes and do like your mother asked you to do. I'm not asking you, I'm <u>telling</u> you. Do it. Now."*

He looked at his mother, as she shrugged her shoulders with a look of non-reproach, looked back at me and said, *"Yes, sir."*

After he changed his clothes, I wished him a good evening and told him I'd see him again at his next class.

As I continued to observe their interactions together at our school, it became clear that he had control of his mother's emotions. She allowed him to make her feel guilty, and it was clear who was in charge.

This young man continued his training for about a year when he reached his first intermediate rank.

When a student moves up to the intermediate level, this is the point where we begin doing more sparring training (the sports aspect of the martial arts) which is like a game of tag with the hands and feet.

Most students love it, but those with less coordination and confidence can sometimes be a little intimidated at first.

He began to miss classes. When I'd ask him where he had been, he made excuses about not feeling well so that mom would keep him home.

I have been teaching for enough years to be able to identify when there is a real issue. When one of my students is struggling with one of the obstacles I mentioned earlier, it's pretty clear.

He began missing classes for a full week, then for a couple of weeks straight.

I called his mother to inquire about his absence, and she replied, *"He just don't want to come no more."*

Since he had been so excited about coming to classes, I asked her why she thought it was that he didn't want to attend any longer. She said she didn't know.

"I just don't want to make him do anything he doesn't want to do," she then said.

I asked her to bring him in so I could speak to him about it.

A couple of days later he arrived in his regular clothes. His formerly-respectful attitude seemed to have disappeared.

We went into the office, and I began by asking questions about his training.

He stared at the wall and, in a monotone voice, he said, *"Yeah, I used to like it, but I don't feel like doing it anymore."*

"Why not?" I asked. *"What changed for you?"*

"Ehh. I just don't like it anymore."

He had also recently won a grand champion trophy at one of our competitions. I remarked how special that was because no one under the rank of black belt had ever accomplished that in our school before.

I was hopeful that his mother would also see this and help me encourage him.

As I was mid-sentence with him, he suddenly turned to his mother and said, *"Can we go now?"*

His mother sat in silence. Rather than correct him for his disrespectful behavior, she allowed him to continue without intervening.

When I realized I was not going to receive any support from mom and that she had allowed him to make his decision, I ended the meeting, and we parted ways.

It's a team effort, and it became clear that *the band was breaking up*.

About six years later, this young man found me on Facebook.

I accepted his friend request but didn't recognize him from his picture. He didn't look like the innocent little boy I once taught.

Instead, his profile picture was a photo of him pointing a handgun gun at the camera.

A few minutes later, he texted me and asked if I remembered him.

He wasn't using his real name, and I couldn't place him.

After a brief conversation, he brought up the incident from my office and apologized for his behavior that day.

He also confirmed my suspicions by admitting that the real reason he quit was that he was afraid of the free sparring.

He then mentioned his disappointment with his mother for allowing him to quit.

Unfortunately, I could tell you many other stories like this one.

BOREDOM

There isn't an activity I can think of that doesn't get boring to a child at some point. Even a day at Disney will *eventually* become dull, and they'll be ready to leave.

Boredom will pass. It's important to remember this when your child tells you that an activity is boring.

Repetition is the mother of mastery, so teaching your child to cope with boredom is a skill that will benefit them in the future. They're going to have to learn to repeat things over and over until they become muscle memory or habit.

To help with boredom, we use a concept in our classes called *disguised repetition.* We work to keep things interesting by mixing up the practice so that it *appears* that they are doing something different. There are many ways to change the focus on the same activity, so that it feels different.

However, monotony is still a small issue, so that is why we break our goals down into even smaller steps. More about this in an upcoming chapter."

There's nothing like a little achievement to revive a child's interest.

Additionally, when they begin to see their skills develop, it tends to re-motivate them.

We also host special events that keep students focused on getting to the next mile-marker on their journey — seminars, social events, graduations, demonstrations, competitions, etc.

Be patient and wait out your child's boredom issues. They will pass.

CONFLICTS WITH PLAYTIME

Younger kids may begin resisting when nice weather arrives, and they want to play with their friends. To avoid having this become an issue, schedule their activities, and stand firm with the schedule.

When a parent has this challenge, we suggest they schedule something less-fun about 30 minutes before it's time to leave for their martial arts class.

That way, the child doesn't mind leaving their chores (for example) and coming to martial arts class.

But, trying to get them out of the swimming pool might be a challenge, because they're already doing something fun.

LACK OF PROGRESS

Students who experience a lack of progress also develop the desire to quit. It's only natural.

That's why we do all that we can to help them see the impacts of little decisions. We expect to see them twice per week. If they miss a week, they have two classes to make up.

If they fail to make up those classes, it snowballs from there, and we end up with an unmotivated student.

To avoid this, we try to stay in close contact with parents to help ensure their child's success.

We teach a straightforward philosophy to students: Take care of the days and the days take care of the weeks/months/years.

It doesn't need to be any more complicated than that.

TOO MUCH FREE TIME

The flipside to having your child involved in an organized activity is to allow them to stay home and do nothing.

Too much free time can be just as wrong as having them involved in too many activities. Here's why:

During my childhood (with all the moving we did) I was surrounded by a lot of kids who negatively influenced me. I got myself into some trouble because of it.

Kids will make friends with other kids who happen to be available at the same time. These might be kids with good morals and values; but why take the chance?

I was what was known as a *latch-key kid*; meaning that when I got home from school, my parents were both still at work, and I had a key to our house.

That meant that between the ages of 7 and 14, I was often home without any supervision.

Without getting into too many details, I'll say that I didn't behave as well as my parents thought I did.

I was friends with other neighborhood kids who also had nothing else going on after school. We met at my house or theirs and got into all sorts of mischief.

One of those days ended with me rushed to the hospital.

My friend and I were shooting at bubble gumballs on the floor with his pump-action B.B. gun.

He pumped the gun until it wouldn't pump any more (for those not in the know, this determines the velocity of the BB).

Then, he aimed at the gumball on the floor.

I was lying down on the other side of the room, waiting for the gumball to get shattered into a million pieces.

Instead, he missed the gumball and shot me in the hip.

I screamed so loudly that my friend (an African-American) lost all the color in his face and temporarily became a Caucasian!

The BB penetrated so deeply that they couldn't remove it without surgery.

The police confiscated his CO2 cartridges and proceeded to let the air out of each of them so that he couldn't use the gun again.

Even though I was in great pain, I couldn't help laughing out loud each time I heard another cartridge emptied of its air...
.........."*FSSSSSSsssssssss.*"

My friend's parents got scolded by the police for leaving the two of us alone at only seven years old.

Nowadays, an incident like that would end up on the news.

Of course, back then, it was also legal to ride in the bed of a pick-up truck on the highway, too!

That was one of many other incidents that could have been avoided had I had a little more supervision.

To this day, that BB still shows up in x-rays.

It makes for an interesting story, but it also serves as a reminder of a poor choice on our parts. I shudder to think about what might have happened if that BB had hit my eye.

When my kids were younger, we lived in a rough neighborhood. I couldn't even allow them to play in our front yard without personally being out there.

Even though it was fenced in, the other kids teased and tried to pick fights with them.

On one occasion, I followed one of these kids to their house to speak to his parents about his behavior. I was greeted rather unpleasantly by the mother when I told her what her son was up to.

She insisted that her son wouldn't say or do these things. She asked him if it was true and he denied it. She then said, "*Well, if my child said he didn't do that, then I have no reason not to believe him.*"

Her attitude towards me was more evidence of the mind-your-own-business parenting style.

Kids who are involved in structured activities are less likely to get involved in situations like that.

FINDING BALANCE

Kids need downtime as much as adults do, but too much can be detrimental to their safety and productivity.

That said, it's crucial to balance your child's activities, so they aren't always on the go.

In our martial arts program, we've seen well-meaning parents have a child in 3 or 4 different activities, simultaneously.

Their schedules are so full that it's a mystery how they fit it all in.

Martial arts classes on Mondays and Wednesdays (and music lessons on the same night). Soccer practice on Tuesdays and Thursdays (and games on Saturdays).

These kids are on the go from sun up to sundown 6-7 days per week.

Their marching band director wants to see them attend some extra training. Their soccer coach wants to see them put more effort into practicing at home. Their martial arts teacher expects the same.

Kids can only do so much in a week and often end up disappointing one or all of them. The result can be loss of self-esteem from disappointing people they respect.

Choose one activity at a time and allow your child time to enjoy a little downtime.

CHAPTER FOUR

✧

The Value of Expectations

THE TURKEYS AND THE EAGLES

A pair of turkeys and eagles were both getting ready to start families at the same time.

The mothers turned to the fathers and told them that they needed to prepare places for their babies to be born.

The father turkey quickly found a bush behind a barn on the farmer's property in which they lived. He brought together some sticks, grass, and brush to create a little nest for the mother to lay her egg in.

On the other side of town, the eagles were having the same conversation.

The father eagle stopped for a moment and carefully considered the best place to build the nest.

He thought, *"I know the perfect place. I'll fly up to the highest mountain where nobody can reach. I'll build the biggest, safest nest a mother eagle could hope for."*

Once the two nests were complete, the mothers sat on their eggs and waited.

When the baby turkey began to peck at the inside of its shell, the mother turkey jumped in excitement!

She began excitedly flapping her wings, running all over the place. She shouted to her husband, "*The baby is coming! The baby is coming! We have to do something!*"

So, papa and mama turkey began pecking at the egg to help their baby break the shell from around himself.

Out popped the baby turkey and he smiled at his parents. They rejoiced at their beautiful baby turkey.

Meanwhile, up in the mountains, the baby eagle began pecking at its shell, too.

Mama eagle jumped in excitement and ran around, yelling (in eagle talk) "*Our baby is coming! Our baby is coming!*"

The parents patiently watched their baby peck at the shell and use his wings to help break it from around himself. That's how the baby eagle develops his wing-strength, just like the butterfly in its cocoon (as you'll learn about in a couple of chapters).

After finally emerging, he spread his wings and smiled at his parents. The eagles were both very excited!

A short while later, back on the other side of town, the baby turkey had begun to notice his wings. He asked his mother, "*What are these things for?*"

Mama turkey replied, "*They are wings, and they are to allow you to fly. But you could get hurt trying to fly, so I don't want you to worry about using them, do you understand?!*"

"*Yes, mommy,*" replied the young turkey.

Up in the mountains, baby eagle began to take notice of his wings, too. He asked his father, "*Dad, what are these things for?*"

The father replied, "*Son, those are your wings, and they will allow you to fly high in the sky and be king of the world.*"

The young eagle emphatically yelled, "*I want to fly!*"

To which the mother replied, "*Be patient son, your father will show you how when you're ready.*"

As time went by, the baby turkey tried using his wings more and more, attempting to get off the ground. Unfortunately, he got fed all sorts of fattening food by his parents and the farmer, so he was too heavy to fly.

Back up in the mountains, the mother had been feeding her baby only the very best food. Food that she hunted and brought back to the nest.

The baby eagle had grown very strong and began peeking over the side of the nest in curiosity.

When the father saw this, he snuck up behind his son and gave him a little nudge.

The baby eagle fell from the nest and cried out for help.

The father eagle yelled down to his son, "*Spread your wings and look up!*"

The baby eagle cried, "*I can't, I'm scared!*"

"You CAN!" yelled his father, *"Now! Before you hit the ground! Spread your wings and look up!"*

As his little body was about to hit the floor of the mountain canyon, he spread his wings as wide as he could and looked up.

The wind caught his wings, and he instantly soared up over the trees and mountain tops.

His father smiled from ear to ear, filled with pride.

His son went on to live a long, healthy life as he became king of the skies and earned the respect of all other creatures.

Back at the farm, the baby turkey had been well-cared for by his parents. They fed him the easiest to find food and made sure he was happy. He grew into a large, round turkey and caught the eye of the farmer.

It had grown late in the year and the month was November. The baby turkey ended up as dinner for the farmer and his family.

Every parent has the choice to parent like the eagles or like the turkeys.

Along with having high standards (as the eagles had), it's important to have equally high expectations (as the eagles had when it came to learning to fly).

If you expect your child to behave, they will behave. If you *expect* them to misbehave, they *will* misbehave.

Children will rise to meet the expectations of the people they are around.

Think of your behavior. Do you behave any differently when you are around someone you respect?

You may have had a grandmother who thought you were better than you were. Because of her high opinion of you, you probably behaved in a way that matched her view.

Like the mother turkey in the story, if you have lower expectations of your child, that's what you can expect.

The eagle parents had higher standards and higher expectations of their child. As a result, the baby eagle thrived. It works the same in real life, too.

Back in 1964, there was a Harvard study done by Robert Rosenthal with two groups of elementary students.

The study was used to determine how important *expectation* from the teachers was to the success of the students.

The basic idea was to discover what would happen if the teachers were told, in advance, that the kids in their class were smarter than the other group.

Rosenthal created a test that he said came from Harvard University, and this test would determine a child's intellectual abilities. Of course, the test he created was phony.

He then selected the students, *at random*, and gave one group to a teacher who was told his students were part of the remedial group.

The other teacher got the supposed group of *gifted* kids.

You can probably already guess what the outcome was.

The kids who took the test with the teacher who had thought they were gifted, scored higher than the other group. The only thing that distinguished the two groups was the *expectations* of the teacher.

I've experienced this in my martial arts classes, and I can assure you it does have an impact.

We named our school *Level 10* Martial Arts College for that very reason.

The term "Level 10" refers to *an Attitude of Higher Standards*. This slogan is prominently displayed and used as a constant reminder to students of our expectations of them.

Level 10 is a rating scale from 1-10; where 1 is your worst effort and 10 is your best effort.

We teach classes with high expectations and continually remind students of this. At each new level, we slightly increase our expectations, as we are preparing them to eventually take the black belt test.

The black belt test is no easy feat. Our curriculum has been carefully designed to test every ounce of a student's ability. When they earn their black belt with us, it is nothing short of life-changing.

Sometimes parents underestimate the potential of their child, and sometimes they can *overestimate*.

As with most things, finding balance is the goal. Start by setting standards that will make your child stretch beyond their comfort zone a bit. Make things challenging but not impossible. Then, gradually turn up the heat as they grow older (i.e., reach a new *level*).

One of the things my master was great at was believing that his students could do incredible things; physically *and* mentally.

On one such occasion, we were at an elementary school to do a demonstration for a group of students and parents. I was a brand new intermediate-level student, meaning that I had about a year of training at that time.

My master was performing to get the audience excited. He showed awesome kicks and lightning-fast weapons skills. Then he turned their attention to us (his students).

First, he had us all line up in formation, and perform some simple basic techniques to help us warm up and get rid of the jitters.

He then sat us down in the back of the room. He called up small groups of students to perform various skills for the audience.

He brought out some pine boards for a couple of students to show the power of breaking boards.

I watched in amazement as a few of my classmates shattered boards all over the cafeteria floor with punches and kicks.

Next, our Master instructed two students to stand side-by-side and hold three 1-inch boards. That meant whoever was going to break was going to have to smash through 3" of solid wood!

I watched in anticipation as my master selected who was going to break these boards.

"James Theros," he said in a very stern voice.

"Yes, sir!" I replied as I rose to my feet with eyes like saucers.

"Back Kick."

It's important to note that I had never broken more than one board before, and I had only recently learned this technique. I began sweating profusely and felt butterflies in the pit of my stomach.

Only one thing gave me the confidence to even attempt this technique, and that was my master's expectations that I could do it.

I let that one thought simmer in my mind for a moment. *"If Master Choi believes I can do this, maybe I can,"* I thought.

I took my stance, gave a loud Kihap (that's the funny yell us Karate guys get made fun of for) and went for it!

To my amazement, the boards shattered into pieces, and the audience erupted in applause.

I grew an inch that day.

THAT is the power of expectation.

CHAPTER FIVE

✧

The Value of Mental Programming

Two primary things will determine the type of person your child will be in the next five years:

1. The Books they Read

2. The People they Associate With

THE BOOKS THEY READ

Number one includes nearly <u>anything</u> they put into their minds.

The human mind is in a constant and never-ending process of being programmed.

The brain is nothing more than a computer system that runs programs; just like your PC or MAC does.

With the right programming, your child's computer will run optimally. If a virus infects it, it will eventually begin to have trouble.

There's an old saying that comes from the computer world of old that applies here…*Garbage in—Garbage out.*

For example, if children are allowed to watch inappropriate movies or television shows, they will be exposed to things that can negatively influence their thoughts and behavior.

A few years ago, I was shocked and appalled to see a very raunchy sex scene displayed on *regular network television* at 7:00 in the evening!

It didn't belong on network television at all, and certainly not on a channel that any child could have tuned in to watch.

These days television stations allow four-letter words in supposedly "edited" TV shows. And many sit-coms on network TV feature filthy language and salty subject matter. These shows are certainly not suitable for children.

The internet is also another denizen for disaster. Pornography is rampant. Companies lure kids to obscene websites by showing scantily-clad women or anime ads (particularly ads for video games).

Video games are another issue all on their own; while not all bad, many of them feature adult language and subject matter.

Music is yet another powerful media that can have a significant influence on a child: many "pop" songs (short for "popular") feature vulgarities and code-words for sex.

Listen *carefully* to the lyrics, and it becomes clear how obscene many of the songs playing on the radio are.

When it comes to music, it's in a parent's best interest to try to keep up with the latest street jargon. Knowing what odd words mean will allow you to understand some of the subject matter your child may be getting exposed to.

Finally, what do your kids hear coming from *your* lips?

When you find it necessary to discipline your child, avoid using profane language. Additionally, avoid language that makes them feel inferior or unwanted.

Always correct their *behavior* (rather than them, as a person). And, if you want to see more of the behavior you like, be sure to praise them when they show it.

Kids who *believe* they are bad, tend to behave badly.

A parent could say, *"I'm grounding you for a week because you've been bad!"*

Or they could say, *"I'm disappointed in your behavior. You're a good child. I don't know why you chose to throw rocks at Mr. Jones' house, but because of your behavior, you leave me with no choice. You're grounded for a week, and you and I will go and visit Mr. Jones. You will apologize to him and offer to pay for the window."*

A child's behaviors will align with their self-image; so helping them develop a healthy self-image is part of a parent's job.

Here's a quick story that happened when my youngest daughter was about 11 years old. I had taken the kids along to a grocery store about 45-minutes away.

On the way home, my oldest daughter told me that my youngest had taken something from the store.

It's important to note that I was already past the half-way mark of our journey home, and we were on a busy interstate.

I pulled off at the first exit, stopped the car and turned to my youngest daughter, who was playing with a little figurine I hadn't seen before.

I asked her where she got it. She looked at me with eyes like saucers and became tight-lipped. She had been busted, and I could see the guilt in her eyes.

I questioned her again, and she slowly said, *"From the store."*

"How? You didn't have any money to buy it," I said.

"I put it in my pocket."

"So, you stole it. I can't believe you would do that. I've raised you better than that. Don't you know that stealing can get you into a lot of trouble?"

The tears came as the guilt further sank in. I then turned the car around, drove back to the store with the groceries getting warm in the trunk. I walked her in and asked to see the manager.

I made her tell the manager why we were there, and she apologized as she handed him the item.

He was very nice about it, and he thanked her for her honesty. He then thanked me for returning the item, and we headed home.

On the way I discussed the event with my daughters and assured them that I loved them, but would not tolerate this kind of behavior.

My youngest learned a valuable lesson that day, one that I'm suspicious she may share with her kids someday.

It would have been much more convenient to yell at her (or handle it when I got back home) because turning around added about an extra *hour* to our trip.

I recognized it as a teachable moment, though.

Whenever you find a teachable moment, take advantage of it....even if it's not at a convenient time or place. It seldom will be.

YOUR CHILD'S CHOICE OF FRIENDS

Your child's choice of friends may be one of the most critical choices he or she makes.

It is *paramount* that your child is surrounded by positive, upwardly-mobile people who will help to bring out their best.

The right people can be a positive influence on your child's thinking and behavior. And the wrong ones can have just the opposite effect.

When I was growing up, I had a few friends who fit into the second category.

Unknowingly, I found myself adopting the attitudes and habits of these friends. I even began using certain words and phrases that they favored.

It wasn't long before I began to get the very same results in school (and at home) that they were getting. The only problem was they weren't getting very good results!

From 1st grade through 5th grade (outside of being a bit of a class clown) I was pretty much an honor roll student.

In my 6th grade year, though, I received my first ever *F* on a report card. In fact, I received 2 or 3 *F's* and a couple of *D's* to go along with them.

I believe this happened for two reasons: My mother finally decided she'd had enough of Ralph, so our family moved a lot that year. Not once. Not twice. But, five times in a single year.

I got so used to being the "new kid" that I didn't have time to make any real friends, and schoolyard bullies were constantly testing me.

That aside, the other (and more important) reason for my poor grades was that I made friends with one particular kid at my new school.

He was obnoxious to the teachers, and mean to kids who were smaller or weaker than him. There never seemed to be a dull moment around him.

I was just glad that he wasn't bullying *me* and that I had finally made friends with one of the "cool" kids.

To make a long story short, he ended up getting expelled from school for the year, and I ended up with poor grades, a poor attitude, and a 3-day suspension.

I firmly believe I would not have had those results had I not become friends with this kid.

Soon after that, my family made our first move of that year, from the small rural town of Whitestown, Indiana to Texas, to live with my Aunt and Uncle for a brief period.

When that didn't work out, we came back to Indiana and temporarily moved in with some of my mother's friends.

As she tried to avoid Ralph, my mother moved us from friend or relative, while trying to maintain a regular work routine.

Finally, my mother and Ralph reconciled and rented a house on the west side of Indianapolis.

I again found myself living in a new neighborhood and going to yet *another* new school.

I continued my poor behavior at this new school and got into more trouble as my grades continued to slide.

Unfortunately, once again, I had made a few new friends at my new school who were not great role models for me.

At this new school, I had a friendly 6th grade teacher, Mr. Tripoldi.

He was a pleasant man who always dressed in a clean, gray suit and wore a hand-tied bow tie.

He *seemed* to be strict but had a friendly demeanor at the same time.

One of my friends assured me that students could talk back to him, and he would make idle threats when they did. He told me how entertaining it was to watch him verbally spar with the troublemakers in his classroom.

A couple of days later, I watched as my friend talked back to him, then mocked our teacher, while the other kids laughed. I couldn't believe my eyes (and ears).

This teacher was allowing my friend to speak to him like a little child. Mr. Tripoldi's go-to response was, *"You better watch yourself, fella."*

He reminded me of the detention teacher in the movie, *The Breakfast Club*. Only Mr. Tripoldi was a bit less intimidating.

I couldn't resist the temptation and looked for an opportunity to test him out for myself.

I couldn't believe what I was being allowed to get away with. I took it to a new level and quickly gained favor with my classmates.

Unfortunately, Mr. Tripoldi was at fault for allowing the students to speak to him the way we did.

If he had been a little bit stricter with us, I would never have even thought to test his mettle.

Fortunately, it was around this time that I started to get serious about my martial arts training. I began going to train with the guy who worked with my mother that I mentioned earlier.

We spent two years at that house before we moved yet again to a house a few miles away.

My mother and Ralph began arguing and fighting again. And this was about the time I met Master Choi.

About a year into my training, I had to move back to Minnesota to live with my father.

I was headed down a dark path and not making wise choices at that time.

When I found Master Choi, things began to change, though. There was something very different about this man.

Master Choi was a principled man who lived by a code of honor. His expectations of his students were very high.

The martial arts became the only stable thing in my life at that time, and provided me with the opportunity to associate with a better class of peers.

In a short time, my outlook on life began to change, and, in particular, my personal view of *authority figures*.

My grades began improving as well, for two specific reasons:

Reason number one was that I was *expected* to have good grades before I could promote in rank in the martial arts. And, since that became very important to me, I started doing better in school.

Reason number two was that I began hanging around kids who *cared* about their grades.

I ended up graduating high school six months early, and I missed the honor roll by one grade (a "c" in *art*, of all things.)

To illustrate how different my life could have ended up, I'll tell you about an old childhood friend from Minnesota who found me on Facebook.

We exchanged phone numbers, and he called me the next day to catch up.

I hadn't seen him in over 25 years. Al I knew was, judging by the pictures on his Facebook page, he looked old! He is two years younger than me, but he looked several years older.

It was apparent that he had lived a hard life since we had hung out together as kids.

During our conversation, I learned that he spent seven years in prison. He got sent there only a couple of years after I had moved from the area. He was arrested and charged for aiding and abetting a murderer!

He's a good man. He's a loving husband and a good father. But, due to the people that he associated with (the same people I was also associating with at one point), his life took a turn for the worse.

He also lost his home to foreclosure and was a laid-off construction worker the last time I spoke with him.

He and I are both fortunate to be alive today, after a few of the stunts we pulled as kids.

One of those stunts involved jumping from rooftop to rooftop in the middle of a Minnesota winter. On one such attempt,

I slipped as I jumped, and fell straight down onto a 3-foot wooden picket fence between two of the houses.

Fortunately, the fence hit my inner thigh, or I may not be here to talk about it.

If you're reading this and you lived in Rochester, Minnesota in 1985 and thought you heard Santa and his reindeer on your roof.... that wasn't Santa....it was my friends and me!

We also hid behind bushes and hopped out to grab onto people's bumpers on the snowy, icy roads. It was known as "skitching," and we literally could have died doing it.

So, stop and think about who your child's friends currently are.

How much do you know about them? And how much time each week is your child spending with each of them?

If you have a funny feeling in your gut about any of them, I would suggest you find a constructive way to remove that child from your child's life.

So, how do you do that?

One of the easiest ways to control who your child is hanging out with is to get them into an organized activity. Choose an activity where they will be around with upwardly-mobile peers with good morals and values.

So, here's another commercial for putting your child into a martial arts program — wink, wink.

CHAPTER SIX

✧

The Value of Learning to Lose

When I was a kid, we had concrete playgrounds, large metal slides, and metal merry-go-rounds that we jumped on with 8-10 other kids and tried to see how fast we could get it moving.... and who could stay on longest.

For games, there was kickball, dodge ball, softball, baseball, tag, football, etc.....

These games had captains who chose teams. There was also a score-keeper to determine a winning team and a losing team.

Unfortunately, many schools have taken out dodge ball because the smaller kids often end up being targets for the bigger kids.

And, some kids' sports organizations have chosen to run scoreless games so that nobody has to be on a losing team. I'm pretty sure the kids still keep score, though.

Playgrounds these days are made of thick foam-rubber, made to *look* like concrete.

This is all well-intended, but it doesn't help kids learn the fine art of falling down (or losing a game)... how to brush it off, and rise up again.

In the real world (the one waiting for kids when they finish their days in school) it doesn't work this way. In the real world, there are winners and losers.

For some reason, we've become hypersensitive to the word "loser." It seems to have become some type of a label, though.

Not everyone who turns in an application will be hired for the job.

Not everyone who tries out for American Idol will get on the show, and of those who do, only one will win.

And, if people perform poorly on their job, they *will* be fired.

Losing doesn't make a person a "loser" in the negative sense of the word. It just means they lost *this* time, and it's ok to lose once in a while. It's actually good to lose sometimes. Losing teaches us humility and perseverance.

From teaching martial arts for so many years, I can tell you that many of today's kids aren't being adequately equipped to cope with losing.

Losing is part of winning. In order to win, long-term, it is a must to learn how to lose.

Learning to deal with failure, or facing a setback, is one of the key ingredients to developing emotional strength. It's also part of developing a healthy self-image and confidence.

One of the key ingredients in baking a cake is eggs. The eggs are what gives the cake its stability. If you leave out the eggs (or whatever else is used as a substitute), the cake would simply *fall apart*.

I've also seen *people* fall apart often because they haven't been taught how to deal with stress that can come from struggle or failure.

Teach your child how to think, and what to say to themselves (and others) when they do lose.

Teach them to keep a positive mindset after a loss and (more importantly) how to look for the silver lining in the situation. The silver lining is often the lesson learned from the failure.

Use Thomas Edison as an example. He was famous for being the inventor of the light bulb. Humanity owes a huge debt of gratitude to Mr. Edison. Without his perseverance and positive attitude, we'd still be lighting lamps and candles at night.

It has been said that he failed over a thousand times before succeeding in inventing the light bulb!

When asked by a reporter how it felt to have failed a thousand times, Edison replied with, *"I didn't fail 1,000 times. The light bulb was an invention with 1,000 steps."*

Talk about a positive mindset! That's what you want to instill in your child.

Try to find healthy ways to think about failure, and what your child should say and do if they fail at something at school or in a sport.

Use your drive time to have meaningful talks with your child to give them some solutions to use when the time comes. Resist the urge to coddle your child when they fail.

Here's another short story to illustrate the point further.

THE BOY AND THE BUTTERFLY

A child was out playing in a meadow and noticed a cocoon. Upon further investigation, he found a butterfly inside the cocoon. He thought he would do it a favor by helping remove it from the cocoon.

This way, the butterfly could emerge without having to fight its way out and could be free sooner and easier.

As the little boy tore open the cocoon and removed the butterfly, it was not able to stand on its own legs. The boy tried to toss the butterfly into the air so that it would fly, but it just fell to the ground.

Shortly after, the butterfly died. It never reached its full potential, never got to experience flight, and never got to fully enjoy the lifespan or the quality of life that other butterflies enjoy.

The little boy meant well, but, rather than helping the butterfly, he actually harmed it.

You see, the struggle to break free from the cocoon is how a butterfly develops its leg strength and wing strength that allows it to fly.

CHAPTER SEVEN

✧

The Value of Self-Defense Training

I'm a big advocate of walking away from trouble whenever possible. I encourage students to find better ways of dealing with an aggressive person than by physical force alone.

Avoidance is only one skill, though.

Children also need to know how to physically protect themselves when avoidance or telling an adult doesn't work.

Sometimes, bullies follow their victims when they attempt to avoid them, and may *force* a child to fight.

One such example happened when I was 14 years old.

The year was 1984. I was in my freshman year of high school and attended a large public school. It had a reputation of being a "tough" school: not academically, but socially. Fights broke out in the hallways nearly every day.

For some reason, one of the school's most notorious bullies (a senior) chose me as his pet that year.

I first noticed him when I'd close my locker and find him staring across the hall at me.

I didn't know who he was yet, but by this time I had already had quite a bit of experience with bullies and new schools. So I knew what was happening.

As I passed by, he said nasty things about me to his friends, loudly enough to make sure that I could hear it.

If I made eye-contact with him, he would ask me (in more-colorful words than this), *"What are you looking at?"*

I just ignored it and continued on my way. After I walked past him, he said, *"You better watch yourself, punk."*

This went on for about four months. The boy sensed I was nervous, which made him grow more confident with each interaction.

One day, as I was on my way to class, I noticed him standing in the restroom doorway. He was holding the door open and motioning me towards him.

"You and me in here, right now," he said in a huff.

I smiled and said something clever, which irritated him further.

I walked past him as a teacher emerged from the classroom and ushered us both on to class.

This went on for another week or two. Same bathroom. Same dare. Same outcome.

He wasn't much taller than I was, but he was more muscular. He probably had a good 15-20 pounds on me. He looked more like a grown man, complete with a full mustache and long, bushy brown hair, and a bit of a beard.

I had heard from my friends that he wanted to fight me because he didn't like me. I was not shy, and I think my personality rubbed him the wrong way. I guess I didn't fit his idea of how a first-year student should behave.

I told my friends that I wasn't too worried about him because I had been training in martial arts for some time.

After a particularly stressful day of school, two of my friends and I were walking home, letting off some steam about the teachers that day.

I was already in a bad mood, so my mindset was a bit more aggressive than usual that day.

My aggressor chose to follow me on my walk home. He brought a friend along with him, and I noticed several older teenagers following him in their car.

He began talking louder and laughing as he and his friend walked behind us a few steps. In a more-colorful way, he was telling his friends how much of a wimp I was.

As I kept walking, ignoring him, he started speaking directly *to* me.

He crept up closer and got louder. As I continued to walk, he started challenging me to fight him, stating that I was too scared. He got louder and grew more animated exclaiming how he was going to destroy me.

I just kept walking.

He had obviously told his friends that today was the day that he was going to force me to fight.

I knew that if I didn't do something, this would continue for the rest of the year. And if news spread that I backed down from the boy, it could even have followed me well into my future years at that school.

As we continued walking, I spoke quietly with my friends and told them that I had had enough of him pushing me around. I was going to stop and fight him.

They tried to talk me out of it. My friends told me how many guys they had seen him beat up, and the stories they'd heard about other kids he'd beaten up. He had a reputation as someone you didn't want to get into a fight with.

They assured me that I was no match for him and told me I should keep walking.

"I don't care," I said. *"I'm not going to take this anymore. I've tried avoiding him for a while now. This guy has to learn."*

I then decided that it was time to "face the music," and I felt something snap inside.

I turned to face him, dropped my books on the sidewalk, and the "go" switch turned on...... and he knew it. I'm sure he saw it in my eyes.

I think it took him by surprise because he hesitated for a moment.

The car with the other boys that had been following us to watch the show quickly pulled up near us.

They began yelling, "Kick his ---!" "Kick his ---!"

My two friends moved away from the action. They wanted no part of the beating I was about to receive.

I told the bully that I was through with him picking on me, and that he chose the wrong day to bother me.

Remembering my training, I took a deep breath and calmed down to prepare to deal with whatever he was going to throw at me.

As he approached to fire off a punch at me, I executed a self-defense technique I had been practicing in my martial arts class.

My body responded with no conscious thought.

I intercepted his punch with a kick that hit his arm and knocked his class ring off his finger. As he ran to retrieve it, I took advantage by chasing after him and landing a flying side kick to his body that knocked him over in the grass.

His buddy (who was wearing cowboy boots) sprang into action and attempted to kick me from behind.

I saw him over my shoulder, turned and blocked the kick and let loose with several spinning kicks to his face.

Both boys backed off in a hurry; exhausted and embarrassed. One was bleeding at the lip, and the other had marks on his body from my strikes, and a torn shirt.

Their friends in the car laughed at them and congratulated me on my victory.

"Nice job, man. You can fight," one of them said.

I grabbed my things and rejoined my friends who were still in awe by what they had seen.

From that day, the bully left me alone. The dirty looks stopped. He went about his business and ultimately paid me no attention. He had been bested by a freshman and his tough-guy reputation was now tarnished. As an unexpected benefit, his friend, who had jumped in to help ended up becoming *my* friend after the altercation.

He told me he respected the fact that I finally stood up for myself.

To this day, I don't regret a thing that I did. I had to learn to physically defend myself because sometimes that's the only thing that works.

Shortly after that, I had to move back to Minnesota, where I would become the new kid once again, and a couple of other similar situations occurred there, as well.

On another note, a second good reason for making sure your child learns how to defend themselves is the all-too-real threat of child abduction.

Although there are many cases, one of them stands out from 2004.

Carlie Brucia, an 11-year old girl from Florida, was abducted by a 37-year old man while she was walking home one evening.

The news released a security camera video showing the man grabbing her by the wrist and pulling her away. She offered no struggle at all.

The attacker had waited until the opportune time to make his move. In the video, it appears that the girl was looking at her phone as he approached her. She can be seen shrinking in fear as he grabs her. They both walk off out of view of the camera and then a couple of other people enter the lot only 7 minutes later.

She was found dead a few days later, only a short distance away from where the abduction took place.

I shudder to imagine how different that situation might have been if Carlie had some self-defense training.

A situation like this could just as quickly happen to your child right in your neighborhood.

Why take that chance?

CHAPTER EIGHT

✧

The Value of Coping with Peer Pressure

Kids should learn healthy ways to respond to the inevitable peer pressure they will experience in school and life. And you are the best person to teach it to your child.

You can probably remember some positive peer pressure moments from *your* childhood. Maybe a friend pressured you into being kinder to others; or showing more respect to your parents or teachers, for example.

I'll bet you can also think of a few instances where negative peer-pressure occurred, too. Being offered a cigarette by a popular classmate, or acting out in class because others were doing it.

Here's something to consider: most of our good habits are the result of someone pressuring us into doing it at first. Brushing our teeth, eating healthy, exercising, going to church, getting to bed early, getting chores done, studying, using the terms sir/ma'am when speaking to elders, etc.

Conversely, most of our *bad* habits came to us without much thought or effort; eating junk food, being late, biting fingernails, being lazy, etc.

Another good reason to make sure your child chooses the right friends to associate with is this idea of good peer pressure versus negative peer pressure.

Kids *will* influence each other, and your child will fall into one of 3 categories: leader, follower, or loner.

Our goal should be to help children grow to be leaders.

So that begs the question, are leaders born? Or are they made? In truth, it's probably a little of both.

If you notice your child displaying signs of being a follower or a loner, there *are* some steps you can take to ensure they have the best chance of becoming a leader.

The first step is verbally reinforcing your child as a leader. At opportune moments, tell your child that he or she is a leader; and that leaders make good decisions.

Teach them about character; character is not just how they think and behave when others are watching; it's how they think and act when they think *nobody* is watching.

If you help your child see themselves as a leader, they will begin to *move* in that direction.

Additionally, coach your child on what to say to a classmate or peer who puts pressure on them.

Try to put yourself in their shoes and understand how they feel. Then, use *feel, felt, found* whenever possible.

Here's how that might sound:

I understand how it <u>feels</u> to want your classmates to like you. I <u>felt</u> the same way when I was in 3rd grade. But let me tell you what I <u>found</u> (tell them an outcome you can remember that helps to illustrate your point).

Teach your child to have high standards; for themselves *and* their friends. Teach them that some friends aren't worth having. A *real* friend would never knowingly attempt to get them to do anything that could bring harm to them.

And having others' approval should be less important than doing the right thing.

After I moved back to Minnesota for the last time, I got reacquainted with a very close childhood friend.

This friend was the toughest and meanest kid in our entire area (probably the whole city).

He was always doing something crazy. Everyone, and I mean EVERYONE, respected and feared him....because nobody could take him in a fight.

We had a few silly, stupid little things we did for entertainment. One of them was making goofy faces to see who could get the biggest laugh.

We'd see who could string together the most adjectives in a row (about what we imagined happened to another student that we teased). We called it *the list*.

Then, we'd read these adjectives off, in a silly voice until the other person died laughing.

It was something we did as 10-year-olds but still found funny.

Well, now we were in high school, precisely five years later.

When I moved back to the area, there were still about four months of school left in the year, and my friend had made friends with the *cool* kids at this school.

He called me over to the lunch table one day to introduce me to his new friends and told them how funny I was.

He told me to read "the list" to them, and I didn't think it would be a good idea since they didn't understand the concept. He assured me that it was ok and that they'd find it hilarious.

I again resisted, and he insisted. So I went ahead and made a fool out of myself in front of these boys.

My friend was laughing hysterically, but the others didn't find it funny at all. They just thought it was weird.

After that, my friend started avoiding me, and we eventually lost touch. His new friends had pressured him into dropping me as a friend because they felt I wasn't cool enough for him.

I made some new friends, and we never spoke again until I found his sister on Facebook about 20 years later.

I was going to be in the area for another friend's funeral, and she put us back in touch. He was very excited about getting back together, and we ended up meeting at a restaurant. It was a blast reminiscing with him about our childhood.

We showed my wife the silly faces, recited some of *the list*, and told stories about the stupid things we did as kids.

He then told me that he was sorry for avoiding me after that day and felt very guilty about it ever since.

He told me how he had allowed his new friends to pressure him into breaking our friendship.

It was unfortunate, but that negative peer pressure caused both of us to lose.

Due to worrying about being popular, and giving in to negative peer pressure time and again, my friend's life at 50 years old sounded like something out of a movie.

He is an alcoholic, works at a dead-end job, and suffers from severe depression.

How different his life could have been had he had only had someone teach him how to respond better to peer pressure.

Maybe you can think of an example from *your* childhood that you could use to educate your child on the dangers of negative peer pressure.

It's very similar to teaching self-defense.

We teach students some of the possible types of attacks (a punch to the face, an attempted choke, a grab to the sleeve, a push, etc.) and then give several methods of dealing with that particular type of attack.

We also cover the "what-ifs." What if plan "*a*" doesn't work? Then what? Plan "*b*" of course (and you should work to actually have a plan "b"), so that when these situations arise, your child is ready.

Do the same for your child in the area of peer pressure.

CHAPTER NINE

✧

The Value of Integrity

Our country was built on integrity. All folks needed in the days of our grandparents was a firm handshake and their word.

Nowadays, in addition to signed contracts, there are voice-recorded verbal agreements. And sometimes these are not enough to get people to do one simple thing.... honor their word.

It seems to be easier to come up with a good excuse than to have to do what they said they would do.

At an early age, I was taught that if I said I would do something to make sure I honored it; plain and simple.

Case in point:

In 2004 I joined a martial arts school located in Chicago, Illinois, to receive some specialized training.

I lived in Indianapolis, Indiana (about 4 hours away).

I drove there every Wednesday to attend a couple of classes and was required to sign a 12-month agreement.

About six months into it, I could no longer keep the commitment of driving up each week.

Rather than canceling my credit card or refusing to pay the tuition I had agreed to, I continued paying until the 12 months were over.

I doubt any court of law would have found me guilty for skipping out on this commitment since I lived in a different state.

It didn't matter though, because I had *agreed* to make the payments. So I honored my word. No complaints on my part. No negative thoughts about them for continuing to charge me each month.

I've sometimes heard parents say, *"He's only five, he doesn't understand yet."*

Guess what? He'll never understand unless you teach him when he's five."

A lot of kids these days are being taught that, if they change their mind (or don't feel like doing it), it doesn't matter what they've promised or committed to.

Excellent education starts at home. Parents must teach kids the value of integrity by insisting they follow through on their commitments.

And, remember it's seldom going to be convenient or comfortable.

Case in point #2:

My youngest son thought it would be fun to be part of a marching band.

When he was accepted, he quickly realized that it meant

many hours of practice in the hot sun. It also meant frequent competitions that would have him gone from sun-up to sun-down on weekends.

It was a bit more of a commitment than he realized at first.

As it started to interfere with his social life, he came to my wife and asked her if she could work some magic to get him out of the program.

She told him that she probably *could* get him out of his commitment but that she wouldn't because HE was the one who made the commitment and had to honor his word.

I'll be the first to admit that it was tough hearing him complain about it for the rest of the season, but it taught him a valuable lesson.

It would have been much easier on us all had she allowed him to quit.

Since we had to attend all of his marching band competitions, we committed along with him.

His mother recognized that he needed to endure that hardship to learn the lesson of integrity.

After that, anytime he was considering committing to something, mom reminded him of his marching band experience.

Whenever he asked about the next thing, she would say, "Is this a marching band thing?"

We need to teach our kids that a handshake and their word is all that's required.

CHAPTER TEN

✧

The Value of Financial Responsibility

If there's one area that my parents could have done a better job, this is it. The only thing I can remember learning about money was that it didn't grow on trees, and we didn't have much of it.

My wife, on the other hand, started teaching our boys about how money worked as soon as they could understand basic math.

She taught them how to save, and helped each of them set up checking and savings accounts while they were still very young.

As business owners, we have conversations about gross profit versus net income (what the business brings in minus all the expenses of running it).

We chose to have these conversations in front of the kids to help them understand how it works and what it all means.

We bought games like Monopoly, Payday, and Life to teach them about finances.

Another game that we recommend is called "Cashflow" (developed by Robert Kiyosaki). It's probably the best game out there to teach finances in a fun, informative way.

Our kids learned all about how to build their credit scores, which was something I had ZERO understanding of before meeting my wife.

As long as I had good enough credit to purchase something I wanted, I was happy. I had no understanding of the bearing my credit score had on so many areas in life.

The higher the credit score, the more trustworthy you appear to banks and lenders (which means you end up paying less in interest).

And, when it comes to purchasing a home, an automobile, or getting capital to launch a business, this can be huge.

When I met my wife, my credit score was in the low 600's. I had no idea what that meant at the time.

Thanks to my wife's financial genius, my score is currently well over 800; as is hers and both of our boys'.

I wish I would have had someone in my life teach me about these things earlier. I would be much wealthier today had I learned about it sooner.

It's never too early to begin teaching your child the value of money and how to make the most of it.

CHAPTER ELEVEN

✧

The Value of Arriving Early and Staying Late

One of my mentors taught me this phrase: *"I'd rather be 30 minutes early than a minute late."*

Everyone is going to be late once in a while, but it should not become a habit. Being late regularly, especially when it is avoidable, can be considered a sign of disrespect.

As a teacher, I can tell you that when a student is repeatedly late, it makes me question how much respect they have for their classmates or instructor.

If it were a job interview, would your arriving late (even if it were just a few minutes) affect the outcome?

It certainly could, so why take the chance, just to enjoy the last few minutes of a television show or some other distraction?

I have a healthy disdain for arriving late for an appointment. I have my father to thank for that. I have always said that he will find a way to be late for his funeral.

My father is a wonderful man. He taught me many valuable things in life. Some of them by proper example, and a couple of them by (ahem) *other ways*. He would laugh at what I'm about to share with you on this subject.

My father has been a musician his entire life. He's what you'd call a true night owl. He generally sleeps all day until early afternoon, rises slowly, and gets going around 5 or 6 pm. He then stays up until about 4 or 5 in the morning.

I lived with him when I was in the 4th and 5th grade, and he was responsible for getting me to school at that time.

I knew he had been up all night and was pretty grouchy when his sleep was disturbed. So I hated waking him when I could see that he was sound asleep.

Finally, I'd get up the nerve to wake him so that I wouldn't be late for school.

When he realized we only had minutes until classes started, he'd throw on his robe, and we'd jump in the car and high-tail it down to the school.

I was late on so many occasions that I lost count.

The kids in my class gave me looks of contempt when I came strolling in, sometimes up to 30 minutes late.

I could tell that my teacher wasn't too happy about it, either; especially when it happened for the second time or third time in the same week.

And to make matters worse, my father, attempting to be funny, would squeal his tires as he left the school. All the kids (and the teacher) knew who it was, and I was always embarrassed by it.

Now, you have to know that my father has always been late for EVERYTHING. He was ALWAYS running late, which included his work.

Fortunately, his *reverse-lesson* was a great gift to me.

I have always tried to be early, and I grow frustrated when I realize I'm running late. I do not make a habit of it.

Consequently, this is also an area that my martial arts master had struggles with. He always told us to arrive early to special events while he showed up 30 to 60 minutes late.

When I became a martial arts school owner, I determined I would not duplicate this habit. I knew how him being late made *me* feel, and I didn't want my students to feel that way towards me!

Being early is being on time; being on time is being late, and being late is rude.

Staying late is also a great habit to develop. It's one way to get the teacher/boss/coach to notice you. If you stick around for a few minutes to see if anyone needs anything, trust me, they'll notice.

When it comes to a job, it could help the employee get a raise or promotion. And when the economy suffers, the first people who get laid off are those who do the minimums.

We want to teach our kids to go above and beyond.

By staying after for a few minutes in our martial arts program, students can either get in some extra practice (which makes them improve quicker) or allows them to help another student (which serves to help both of them- because when one teaches, two learn).

CHAPTER TWELVE

✦

The Value of Reading

Of all the success skills you teach your child, teaching them to enjoy reading is on my list of the top 3.

"Leaders are Readers" is one of my favorite childhood quotes, and I believe it still applies today. Nothing against audiobooks and podcasts (because they are both excellent), but nothing beats turning pages, dog-earing them, and marking up a book with highlighters and personal notes.

Teach your child to enjoy reading, by first reading *to* them, and then encouraging them to read on their own.

Start with storybooks that have morals to them, and then buy them educational books to teach them things in areas that you may not have enough experience or knowledge.

I'm always amazed to hear people say that they stopped reading once school was over.

For successful people, school is never over. Their teachers just become more two-dimensional (i.e., books).

Reading is one of the best ways to learn from some of the smartest minds who ever lived. And with public libraries, it's even free.

I still recommend helping your child develop a library of books that they *own*.

Author and speaker, Jim Rohn was famous for saying, *"Poor people have big TVs, rich people have big libraries."* I couldn't agree more.

It wasn't until I was in my early 20's that I got reintroduced to the concept of reading for education. It turned out to be one of the very best recommendations of my life.

I started with thin, easy-reading books, and after several of those, I graduated to thicker ones. I eventually learned to enjoy novels and self-help books of 1,000 pages or more.

So, it was a *process*. I didn't just start reading thick, difficult to understand books right off the bat.

I'm still not a very fast reader and often have to read the same paragraph a couple of times to understand and comprehend. But I strive to do at least some reading every day of the week.

I will often read one chapter of a book per day. When I'm reading two or three books simultaneously, I will read three pages per day from each.

Think of reading as *food for the mind*. Reading has many positive benefits: better vocabulary, thought stimulation, and memory improvement to name just a few.

A great series of books to start with are by author, Og Mandino:

- The Greatest Miracle in the World

- The Greatest Salesman in the World

- The Greatest Secret in the World

- The Choice

- The Twelfth Angel

- The Greatest Success in the World

CHAPTER THIRTEEN

✦

The Value of Setting Goals

It's never too early to begin helping a child learn to set goals. After all, it's the foundation of all success.

As mentioned in a previous chapter already, traditional martial arts training can assist in the area of goal setting like few other activities I know of.

When it comes to setting goals, there are four primary areas to consider:

1. Personal

2. Family

3. School/Career

4. Finances

Parents should consider teaching their children how to set goals in each of these areas. So, what if you never learned to set goals, yourself?

I say, there's no time like the present. And, here's something else to consider: anytime you begin teaching something to another, you will start learning more about that subject, yourself.

I assure you that if you aren't where you had hoped you'd be in life, goal-setting (or lack, thereof) has something to do with it.

As the old saying goes, "It's never too late to become the person you were meant to be."

There are a few things to know about the basics of goal setting. The first thing is to make sure that your goals are S.M.A.R.T.

S= Specific

M= Measurable

A= Attainable

R= Realistic

T= Timely/Tangible

Specificity: Your child's goals must be specific. The more specific, the better. So, what kinds of goals might a child have between the ages of 4 and 7?

Getting good grades might be one of them. Making friends with another child who doesn't seem to like them could be one. Saving up enough money to buy a nice gift for mom or dad could be one. Saving up enough money to buy a specific toy they want could be another, developing a particular skill (jumping higher, running faster, doing the splits) or making their parents proud, etc. These are all goals that kids might have.

Measurability: Your child's goals need to be able to be measured. So, when helping them set their goals, be sure to consider this. If there isn't a way to measure it, the goal has not been clearly-defined enough.

For example: if the goal is to save money, can that be measured? The answer is yes; if a specific amount is set. Simply saying, "saving money" isn't specific enough to compel a person to stick to the goal.

Attainability: This is one area that many people who set goals make a mistake. Setting the goal of saving a million dollars, while a lofty goal, is probably a bit unattainable for many.

However, setting the goal to save $1000 could be a starting point that a person could achieve. When the person gets closer to the target, a new goal can be $2,000 or maybe $3,000.

Since this is much more attainable, the person is more likely to stay committed to the habit of saving money.

Timely: Rather than leaving a goal open-ended, with no real time-frame in which you want to achieve it, it's essential to include a specific time-frame.

For example, staying with the saving money theme, the goal would be more-likely achieved if it were to save $1000 by June 30th of next year.

The S.M.A.R.T. system can work for *any* goal. The first step, though, is to have some goals to achieve. Stop and ponder how much further you might have gone by setting goals earlier on in your life.

Sit down with your child and start the dialogue about who they want to become in the next 12 months. What personal goals should they set? Maybe they want to start eating healthier foods, getting more rest, making new friends.

For family goals, it could be that they want to begin being more-helpful at home, or be kinder to their sibling, or adopt a pet.

For their school goals, it could be getting on the honor roll, getting on the principal's list, getting straight A's, getting perfect attendance.

For their financial goals, maybe they'd like to save enough money for a new toy they'd had their eye on for a while.

Did you know that one of the very *best* skills learned through martial arts is the skill of setting and achieving goals?

In the martial arts, we help beginner students set the goal to achieve their black belt; which generally takes about four years.

Then we break that long-term goal down into smaller, achievable goals. We accomplish this through the use of a colored-ranking system (the martial arts belt) that helps them see *visual progress* towards the attainment of the first milestone in martial arts: the black belt.

The student then breaks the smaller goals of each colored belt down into even *smaller* steps.

To keep students on track, we have them earn a set of *achievement stripes.*

The achievement stripes are little pieces of electrical tape (earned when a student learns one of their requirements for promoting in rank).

We make the process progressively more challenging as they rise higher in rank.

Then, we teach them the proper responses to the emotional and mental stress that goes along with achieving any worthwhile goal.

In the end, they learn *so* much more than just how to defend themselves in a physical fight.

There are four basic levels in the martial arts. These levels (or phases) are beginner, intermediate, advanced, and expert.

Each phase lasts approximately 12 months; which allows a student to focus on completing one year at a time as they ascend the ladder of achievement.

We teach the skill of goal-setting in great detail; starting with the belt and stripe system mentioned earlier.

We don't stop there, though.

Many classes are used to teach the students how preparing to earn their next rank directly applies to getting better grades, saving money, losing weight, or achieving virtually any other goal.

At the beginning of each year, we spend the entire month of January fully-immersed in how to set and achieve goals (and why new year's resolutions never work).

Simply put, successful people are goal-setters, and goal setters are goal-*getters*.

CHAPTER FOURTEEN

✧

The Value of Being a Parent First

When it comes to parenting, it can be easy to get caught up in caring more about how much your child likes you than enforcing proper behavior.

Here's a common situation that occurs when parents get divorced:

One parent pits the child against the other.

A mini-war begins between the two parents. They use the child as some sort of *weapon* to get back at the other.

We've seen one parent be very excited about having their child in our program, while the other thinks it's the worst decision ever.

And guess what? When that happens, it's tough for the child to excel in our program. It's like driving with one foot on the gas and the other on the brake.

In many families, one parent is the disciplinarian, and the other the nurturer. One thinks the other is too hard on the child, the other not hard enough.

It's essential to find balance and to realize each parent's role in raising the child.

In the case of divorced parents, remember that your child is watching and learning from you. Each "dig" you dish out is being picked up by your child.

The child may not even realize what's happening at the moment, but as they grow older, they will begin to understand what took place.

It can be a cause for resentment later on.

Sometimes you have to make the hard calls for your child, and your child may not "like" you for it. So be it. You've probably had a time or two where a boss made a decision you didn't like, either.

I remember my daughter trying to pressure me into buying her a new phone, and when I told her no, she called me a "bad dad."

I wasn't her friend that day, nor was I her friend when I made her return the stolen item to the grocery store that day.

She didn't need the phone. I told her if she wanted it she'd have to pay for it herself, and that didn't make me too popular with her that day.

When we've caught our kids in a lie, we confronted them and called them on the carpet for it. Not fun. Not easy. Not the best way to make them like us.

Didn't matter. Nor should it.

I can still remember a day back when I was about eight years old.

I did something that I shouldn't have done, and then I lied about it. My mother knew right away that I had lied to her because the evidence was too difficult to conceal.

I had invaded her change jar and loaded my pockets with quarters to play video games at the local arcade, and my pockets were bulging.

She asked me if I had taken money out of the jar, and I denied it.

She calmly told me to head back upstairs.

What happened next changed my behavior forever.

Now, you have to know something about my mother; she's not one to stay calm when she's upset. She's downright scary.

She told me to lie down on the bed, face down, and not move. Then, she proceeded to whip my lying behind until I cried.

There was no anger in her swings. She was not shouting at me as the belt struck my behind. She just swatted until she felt I had learned my lesson.

Now, you may think I had a reason to not like her after that. And for a brief moment, I didn't.

When she finished disciplining me, she calmly told me that she didn't raise a thief.

Her words stung more than the belt because she was right; I was wrong. On top of that, I had lied to her.

After about an hour or so thinking about what I had done, I went downstairs, apologized, gave her a big hug, and told her I loved her.

I deserved that spanking, and she did what she was supposed to do as a parent: enforce proper behaviors with her son. It was a teachable moment.

I never forgot that lesson.

A parent's job is to raise a child; not to be best friends with them.

Sometimes, that will mean that you have to be okay with them not liking you.

As a martial arts instructor, I could choose to be easy on my students and focus on making sure they're having fun and that they like me. If I did that, I'd probably have twice as many students and make twice as much money.

The problem, though, would be that they wouldn't develop the proper skills needed to flourish as martial artists.

At times, I'm downright hard on them, but I always let them know that I do it out of love and that I love them. I care enough about their future to be hard on them when I see them underperforming.

After teaching thousands of students, I've become reasonably adept at determining student-potential.

When I see a student suddenly "get it" or start doing something they didn't do as well before I make a HUGE deal out of it.

I let them know that I'm an equal-opportunity teacher. I'm hard on them, but I equally praise them when they do well.

While I don't allow them to overstep their boundaries, I make a conscious effort to show them that I'm friendly, too.

I make them earn every accolade they get in our school. From their rank down to a small compliment. That way they know that they've truly earned it and deserve it.

They aren't always happy with me, but they know I care about them and about seeing them reach their full potential.

As a parent, if you handle things properly, your child will love you *even more* later on.

You can be their *friend* when they reach adulthood, once they have developed the morals and values that you are obligated to instill in them. Until then, be their parent. Their future depends on it.

Be consistent. Be persistent. Be patient.

In closing, I'd like to include some of the things that are on the walls of our martial arts school that may give you some ideas to use at home.

THE 10 ARTICLES
OF MENTAL TRAINING

1. Be Loyal to your school and country.

2. Be Obedient to your parents.

3. Be Respectful to your elders.

4. Be Cooperative between brother and sister.

5. Be Faithful between friends.

6. Be Faithful between teacher and student.

7. Be Honest in your personal affairs.

8. Be Helpful to the weak.

9. Never Kill anything with a reason.

10. Always Finish what you start.

CHILDREN'S HOME RULES

1. Show respect to parents and family members at all times.

2. Greet parents when entering the house and tell them goodbye when leaving.

3. Be truthful at all times.

4. Maintain good relationships with brothers and sisters.

5. Help with household chores.

6. Keep your own room clean.

7. Clean your body, teeth and hair every day.

8. Do not interrupt adult conversations.

9. Study your school work at home and at school.

10. Show respect for teachers and peers at all times.

THE STUDENT CREED

1. I will avoid anything that would reduce my mental growth or physical health.

2. I will develop self-discipline to bring out my true potential and inspire others through my example.

3. I will never abuse my training.

AFTERWORD

✧

I want to thank the following people for helping me assemble the material in this book.

First and foremost, I'd like to thank my wife, Debi. She is the quintessential mother and wife. She's taught me many things about how to raise children with strong morals and values. She is who I credit for my success; as a father, as an instructor, as a businessman, and as a man. I always had the potential, but she provided the key to unlock that potential.

Secondly, to my parents, James and Billie Jo, for raising me and doing the best that they could to provide me with the tools I needed to succeed in life.

Thirdly, to Grandmaster Young Pyo Choi for being my second father, and the man who influenced me more than any other man in my life.

And, finally, to all of the students and families of Level 10 Martial Arts College.

Thank you for allowing me to learn from the many wonderful families that have been part of our program over the years.

Watching you raise your kids has helped me become a better father, instructor, and leader.

ABOUT THE AUTHOR

✧

James Theros is the parent of 4 children, and a father-figure to thousands of other children, through his work as a professional martial arts instructor.

James was born in Indianapolis, Indiana in February of 1969. He is the oldest of 3 siblings. With a background as a martial arts instructor, he has had the privilege of witnessing some of the most effective methods of raising children, as well as observing the results of some less effective ways of parenting.

Through interactions with children and their parents, James has been able to glean the most commonly-used methods of many of his student's most successful parents.

Master Theros has often been called a "stern but loving parent" by his students.

He receives testimonials from parents of children that he has worked with on a regular basis.

"It is a parent's responsibility to raise their children with respect, honesty, patience, and integrity. These qualities are important for young men and women of all backgrounds. When a parent tries to instill these qualities on their own, but feel as if they are falling short, it is important to know there is a place where they can go for help. For our family, this was Level 10 Martial Arts College. My son, Tyler, is a good kid who was struggling in school. He had just been diagnosed with ADD and was having a very difficult time following through on some of the processes he needed to assist his

learning. From day one, James Theros and his wife, Debi made him feel like he was a confident person who could accomplish anything. They gave him a confidence that I had never seen before.

Martial arts may be known by many as punches and kicks but for Level 10 it is so much more. Their teaching is a standard of higher learning. Thus, their school is a martial arts college and not simply a karate school. This is evident in every small detail. Students are taught not only punches and kicks but also lessons that that will serve them well now, as well as, later in life. In addition, as a parent I have also learned so much more about my son that I did not see before. Due to the teachings at Level 10, Tyler was able to improve his focus, confidence, and attention to detail going from a below-average student to an average to an above-average student in many subjects.

There is so much more I can say about this school but the truth is nothing can truly be understood until it is experienced and it is with the utmost admiration that I would recommend Level 10 Martial Arts College to anyone who is looking for a quality school that cares about the student above all.

-Sheryl Pelletier